Introduction

The great feast of the Nativity of Our Lord (Christmas) is preceded by the Advent season. This prayerful time of reformation and rejoicing begins on the First Sunday of Advent, which can be as early as November 27, or as late as December 3. When Advent is early, Christmas may not be celebrated until the end of the fourth week of Advent, and so this booklet has four complete weeks of daily reflections, as well as ones for Christmas Eve and Christmas Day. The theme that is heard throughout these Advent reflections is the clarion call of Isaiah and John the Baptist for us to become laborers who prepare the road to Christmas so that Christ will be born once again in us for the sake of our world.

> O God,
> Grant me your grace as I take up my
>   Advent shovel
> to fill in the valleys of neglect
> in my prayer and daily life.
> May I be zealous in my labors
> of straightening out the crooked
> ways
> and leveling the mountains and hills
>   of sin
> and false contentment
> that block the coming of Christ.
> Amen.

The First Sunday of Advent

Our Advent theme song:
"Hi Ho, Hi Ho, it's off to work we go."

Vividly tattooed in my childhood memory is that scene from Disney's *Snow White* where the seven dwarves tromp off to work with picks and shovels over their shoulders singing, "Hi Ho, Hi Ho, it's off to work we go." Just as appropriate as singing "O Come, O Come, Emmanuel" on this first Advent Sunday, we could join in that happy work song of the seven dwarves. Advent's foreman, John the Baptist, shouts, "Shoulder your pick and shovel, and go make straight your crooked ways; fill in your valleys and level your mountains—prepare the way of the Lord."

Advent's assignment includes both being *more* and being *less:* carving out space in our mountains of commitments for prayer and Advent reflection, filling up the low levels of our generosity, and reducing old Mount Self-Indulgence so we can prepare a path for the Lord. Break your Sabbath rest today! Go to work on preparing the way and do so like the seven dwarves—joyfully!

Monday of the First Week of Advent

Fear is a crooked road.

Monday in the first week of Advent is haunted by the spine-chilling predictions in Sunday's gospel about imminent calamities and the apocalyptic end of the world. We hear echoes of those dark warnings in our daily news, which is filled with fear-inducing reports of war and genocide, rampant hunger and disease in developing nations, violence and corruption in our cities and towns, abuse and neglect in our schools and homes and places of work. The FBI reports that every fifteen seconds thieves break into an American home. Today it may be yours.

But the gospel bids us to fear not. Crooked and warped becomes the way of the fearful who doubt God's abiding care. This Advent let us use the pickax of Jesus' words to chip away at our fears and walk a straight path of trusting in God's encompassing care. Whenever fear twists and distorts our pathway, we can repeat Jesus' promise: "Do not be afraid for I am with you always—and everywhere."

Tuesday of the First Week of Advent

Advent acrobats are like rubber bands—
flexible and elastic so that they can
keep their balance.

A dvent has us living a double life: one in church anticipating the birth of Jesus on Christmas Day—and the other celebrating a holiday season that has already arrived. For most, it's not the roadwork of preparing a way for the Lord that is uppermost on our to-do lists, but rather the homework of decorating indoors and outdoors, wrapping gifts and preparing for family celebrations. We're more involved in putting up Christmas trees than bringing down mountains that block the way to Christ's birth in us and our families.

Living in our world and being faithful to a holy Advent does not have to leave us spiritually conflicted. Rather, it can challenge us to become Advent acrobats. Advent offers us spiritual twins: celebrating Christ who has already come, and patiently waiting for his rebirth in us and his coming in glory at the end of time. Let the twins call you to be an Advent acrobat skillfully balancing the roadwork of spiritual reconstruction with the homework of festivity: a two-lane path of preparing for Christmas.

Wednesday of the First Week of Advent

The soft life and sleeping sickness smother the Spirit.

Jesus warns against obesity! He cautions us not to be bloated by soft living, too much luxury, or so emotionally weighted down that it is difficult to work on the needs of our inner life. As disciples of the Way, we cannot afford to be arrested for DWI, "discipling while under the influence." Disciples drunk with excessive concerns about their day-to-day needs lack energy for the work of reconstructing their hearts. To these warnings Jesus adds, "Beware of sleeping sickness. Stay awake. Be constantly on the watch."

Any of us who nap through life are guilty of the sin of presumption: taking our loved ones, home, health, and every good gift for granted. Live today in an Advent state of being perpetually awake and you'll find your way crowded with intoxicatingly beautiful gifts, rich beyond all imagining. In recognizing even your passing gifts as priceless, you will catch a glimpse of those that are permanent.

Thursday of the First Week of Advent

"Now is the hour for you to wake from sleep."
—Paul of Tarsus

Advent is a time for anticipating the Second Coming of Christ as well as the coming of Christ in you personally and in our society at large. At the same time, we prepare to celebrate the holy birth of long ago. This is an enchanted season with past and future collapsing into the present, but you don't have to be a child to be awestruck by its splendor. It's not just midnight on Christmas Eve that seems magical, but each joyous hour is like a sleight of hand in which the future vanishes. While time is now measured in nanoseconds—one-billionth of a second—we continue to "tomorrowize." We procrastinate into the future the changes we need to make in our behavior and lifestyle today.

The Advent Jesus says, "Be on guard . . . you do not know when the Master is coming . . ." Advent clocks do not have hours, minutes, or seconds; both hands point only to now, the present moment. This very moment is the time to pick up your Advent pick and shovel and make straight the way of the Lord.

Friday of the First Week of Advent

"They shall beat their swords into plowshares
and their spears into pruning hooks . . . "
—The prophet Isaiah

Have you not at some time longed to do something about the suffering in the world? The earth agonizes from its gaping wound that festers from war and hatred, disease and starvation, the miseries of poverty, and vast abuses of the human spirit. World leaders and religions all seem unable to heal the wounds. Only God can bring peace to the world and rescue those in need. So we pray that God sends peace and healing.

But is prayer really enough? What more must we do?

In the reading for mass on this first Friday of Advent, Isaiah says, "But a very little while and Lebanon shall be changed into an orchard . . . on that day . . . the lowly will find joy and the poor rejoice." The Koran adds, "God changes not what is in a people until they change what is in themselves." Change is the work of Advent, and that change isn't merely spiritual reform. The crooked ways of the world are straightened as you and I change our lives, share our goods with the needy, and convert our household weapons of arguing and angry silence into creative tools of love.

Saturday of the First Week of Advent

"in hoc signa vinces—in this sign you shall conquer."
—Motto of the Emperor Constantine,
fourth century

When the work of smoothing out whatever is rough and rugged in your personal landscape seems too daunting, ponder the art on the cover of this booklet. The ancient Christian symbol Chi-Rho is formed by the crossed handles of the two shovels intersecting with the "I" of the upright handle of the pick. This is one form of the XP, the first two Greek letters of *Christos*, "Christ." It is a sign of victory. The Roman emperor Constantine led his troops victoriously into battle with a long gold spear on which was attached a purple banner inscribed with the Chi-Rho and the words *in hoc signa vinces*, "in this sign you shall conquer."

Whenever you're tempted to abandon Advent's hard construction work of smoothing out the rough ways, make the sign of the cross upon yourself and return to the work of making this the happiest and holiest Christmas of your life. As this week ends, remember how it began—with the song of the seven dwarves. While Lent is a somber, penitential time, Advent is filled with joyful anticipation. So, "Hi Ho, Hi Ho, it's off to work we go."

The Second Sunday of Advent

"Every act of compassion and kindness
cleanses away the effects of your past actions."
—Ancient Asian proverb

John's baptism required a confession of sins, and so Advent is traditionally a time for examining our conscience and seeking forgiveness of our sins. To make ready the way of the Lord requires escaping from the effects of habitual failings that can ensnare us like tangled vines and hold us back from truly living our faith. To those crippled by their sin Jesus declares the good news of an existing reality, "Your sins are forgiven!" God "be-for-gives," granting us mercy before our sorrow is even expressed. Jesus reveals this in his story of the prodigal son, who was forgiven by his father even before he could confess his sin.

Although our sins are forgiven, their side effects may be like clinging vines that can continue to shackle us. This Second Sunday of Advent is a good day to examine your present behavior for any lingering effects of past failings. After this examination, you can begin untangling yourself by practicing the opposite of your sins: Substitute generosity for greed, honesty for deceit, love for prejudice, self-giving for selfishness, and trust for mistrust.

Monday of the Second Week of Advent

"Mary, know that you have found favor with God and that you shall conceive and bear a son . . . Jesus."

—The Angel Gabriel, Gospel of Luke

The pregnant Madonna is the Queen of Advent. Mother Mary is a beautiful mirror image for each of us who desires to be pregnant with Christ. The work of Advent is really life-long, reflecting the birthing pains of Mary ready to bring Christ into the world. Likewise, as our Advent labor becomes more intense, the reality of Christ in our lives becomes more and more apparent. With a childlike eagerness for the arrival of Christmas, let us be eager to bring forth the living Christ into our homes, our churches, our neighborhoods, and our nation.

Just as a blessedly bewildered Mary questioned how God could bring forth the Christ from within her, we too might question that same mysterious birth in us. And, like Mary, we too have the freedom to decline God's invitation. It does, after all, involve a great deal of labor pain and suffering. This week, whenever you sense the impossibility of Christ being born anew in your life, recall the angel Gabriel's words, " . . . nothing is impossible for God."

Tuesday of the Second Week of Advent

God loves detours, so be prepared to change course.

"Hail Mary, full of grace!" This is our prayer saluting Mother Mary, who was full of the grace that allowed God to work wonders in her life. Mary was engaged to Joseph when her angelic visitor delivered God's invitation for her to change course, to detour along a different way. *Detour* is an Old French word meaning, "to turn away," and Mary's way was a roundabout way, not the main route. Becoming pregnant before marriage was a deviation from the usual way, and like it did with Mary, life often takes us to unexpected places by unexpected routes.

Whenever you are forced to change your path, don't curse the detour signs, but pray for the grace to say with Mary, "I am the servant of the Lord; let it be done to me as you say."

Wednesday of the Second Week of Advent

"'Tis grace has brought me safe thus far,
and grace will lead me home."

—From "Amazing Grace" by John Newton

If we've been faithful to the roadwork of Advent, we've increased our good deeds, our gifts to the poor, our prayer and devotion. Today's Advent assignment is to tattoo on our minds the reality that all our generosity, prayerfulness, and forgiveness are possible only because of the gift of God's grace. We can be justly proud when we cooperate with those divine gifts, but we need to remember that even our collaboration with grace is a gift of grace.

Christmas is the season of gift giving, so we are called today to marvel in wonder at the avalanche of God's gifts of dynamic energy. While we work at leveling our mountains of self-importance—which may have taken years to reach their height—our Advent song calls us to wonder while we work. Be in awe that working in and through you is God's awesomely amazing grace, leveling your old Pride's Peak.

Thursday of the Second Week of Advent

"Against our will, comes wisdom to us by the awful grace of God."

—Aeschylus, 5th century Greek dramatist

The hymn "Amazing Grace" sings of the sweet, precious grace that changed a sinner's ways. Today calls us to ponder not the "amazing" but the "awful" (awe-filled) grace of God. Aeschylus was the first to introduce scenery into plays, and he also wrote the first tragedies. Daily life is a stage set within the scenery of your home and workplace that occasionally involves heartbreaking tragedies, some minor and some not. A favorite dish is broken, a child is arrested, or the threat of cancer is discovered. There are also the personal tragedies of our mistakes, misjudgments and sins that bring misfortune but also wisdom to those who are students of failure.

"Amazing Grace" declares, " 'Tis grace that's brought me safe thus far, and grace will lead me home." Amazing is the gift of awe-filled grace that offers the wisdom to lead us home to God.

Friday of the Second Week of Advent

"I find letters from God dropped in the street,
and every one is signed by God's name."

—Walt Whitman

Besides the spiritual roadwork of straightening out our crooked ways, this is the time of year to write greetings to family and friends. Imagine a Scrooge-like person who never opened a single one of his Christmas cards! When asked why, he would reply, "Bah humbug! I'm too busy!" Advent is perhaps the busiest time of the year, with all the activities of preparing for Christmas. Being too busy blinds us to many things, such as those letters Whitman found scattered in his path. Consequently, a critical part of making a holy path is clearing away the blinding debris of our hectic activity so we can see—and have time to open—the letters God has left for us to find.

Creation as well as church, city streets as well as stores, schools and workplaces as well as homes, are all one giant mailbox. Open, and read, your mail!

Saturday of the Second Week of Advent

"The best way out is always through."
—Robert Frost

Robert Frost provides excellent Advent advice for making straight the way of the Lord. When you find your way blocked by a wall or some seemingly immovable obstacle like a mountain, don't try to go around it; rather plunge right through it. John Kennedy quoted an old adage: "When you're out walking and you come upon a wall blocking your path, throw your hat over the wall and then go get your hat." Just so, you can throw your heart over your seemingly impassible walls of heartache and sin and then set out to retrieve your heart.

The 13th century mystic and poet Rumi said, "Be grateful and welcome difficulty. Learn that the moment you accept what troubles you've been given, the door opens." That door is the gate of heaven, out of which flows all kinds of magnificent gifts. So, be grateful if today you find that your path is blocked.

The Third Sunday of Advent

"Rejoice always and give thanks constantly."

—Paul of Tarsus

John the Baptist's stern Advent reform is balanced by the pervading spirit of merriment and joy created by the nearness of Christmas. In the midst of a festive atmosphere of wrapping gifts and having parties, it is easy to "rejoice always." However, continuously rejoicing requires something more. When asked his opinion of John the Baptist, Jesus pointed to the source of true and everlasting joy. After saying that history had not known a greater man than John, he said, "Yet the least born into the kingdom of God is greater than he."

His words have staggering implications for those of us who are able to live out our baptism into the kingdom. This third Sunday of Advent calls us to true rejoicing, for our Advent roadwork opens the way for Christ to birth in us the fullness of God's kingdom.

Monday of the Third Week of Advent

"When giving gifts do not let your left hand know what your right hand is doing."

—Jesus of Nazareth

Christmas is the Feast of Giving, and so our purchasing, wrapping, and giving of gifts need to become part of our Advent roadwork. Shopping can be fun or it can be a nightmare, if the dilemma of what gifts to pick out or how to pay for them overwhelms us. Yet easily overlooked in the pleasure or dread is the secret of how to make gift-giving a joyous art! Perhaps Professor Santa Claus teaches us, as children, the first lesson of this art: Give gifts secretly (while all are asleep), and then run away before you can be thanked. Master Jesus teaches us the second lesson: Whenever you give a gift, suffer instant amnesia—be a "forgifter" by not letting your left hand know what your right hand is doing. Forgetting your gifts causes the need to be thanked to vanish.

Practice the art of giving gifts secretly and absent-mindedly this Christmas. It will give you the gift of becoming more God-like, which is the very purpose of Advent.

Tuesday of the Third Week of Advent

"A great sign appeared . . . a woman clothed
in the sun,

with the moon at her feet, and on her head
a crown of twelve stars,

. . . she was with child. Then another sign
appeared . . . a huge dragon,

flaming red . . . and his tail swept a third of the
stars from the sky."

—Revelation

Advent joy finds expression in the Fiesta of Our Lady of Guadalupe, which celebrates the dazzlingly sun-clothed Madonna, crowned with twelve stars. John's splendorous vision becomes ominous with the appearance of a great, flaming-red dragon that seeks to devour the child about to be born. While such horrible dragons are absent from our Christmas legends, you can easily entertain guest dragons during the holidays. The old abbot at the Benedictine abbey where I studied was fond of saying, "The greater the feast, the more active in the monastery is the devil." The same may be true for your home.

As Christmas draws near, issue a "Dragon Alert" in your home. Be on guard for invasions by the fiery dragons of anger and resentment and for sneak attacks by the juvenile dragons of impatience, rudeness, and pouting. Take up your Advent pick and shovel and be on guard.

Wednesday of the Third Week of Advent

"By means of all created things, without exception, the divine assails us, penetrates us, and molds us."

—Pierre Teilhard de Chardin

God, assuming the fullness of humanity in the person of Jesus, is the awesome mystery of Christmas that inspired the carol, "O come, all ye faithful. Come let us adore him." As wondrous as this reality is, God did not mean for this enfleshment to stop with the person of Jesus. What God intended is for all of us to know the gift of Christmas mirrored in ourselves. What joy it is to realize the words of Teilhard de Chardin, "Without exception . . . the divine . . . penetrates us." There is no better preparation for Christmas than to personally embrace this incredibly stunning reality. Isaiah, who began Advent by calling us to make straight our crooked ways, had a vision of creation penetrated by the divine and cried out, "Holy, Holy, Holy . . . heaven and earth are filled with your glory."

Let the impending feast of Christmas be for you an eye opener each time you look out a window—or into a mirror.

Thursday of the Third Week of Advent

*"For where God built a church,
there the devil would also build a chapel."*
—Martin Luther

As you rejoice in how you've straightened out your Advent roadway, be alert and cautious for any obstacles thrown across your freshly cleared path. Interestingly, the Greek word for devil, *diabolos*, literally means, "to throw across"—as when something is thrown out to block your path. Nose-to-the-grindstone Christians often say that "idleness is the devil's workshop." But pre-Christmas hustle-bustle and hurry-hurry could be the devil's favorite laboratory for mischief. In fact, one of the best ways to prepare the Way is to be idle!

Carve out small islands of quiet in the midst of your mountain of helter-skelter activities. You need it to clear your path so that you can see clearly and avoid tripping over the obstacles thrown in your way. These stumbling blocks come less from outside evil forces than they tumble forth from within the dark, unredeemed parts of us. Watch your step, as Martin Luther warned, for within this godly shrine of Advent the devil also wants his chapel.

Friday of the Third Week of Advent

"O Christmas Tree! O Christmas Tree!
You stand in verdant beauty."

—German folk carol

By now most homes are fully decorated for the holidays, with a colorfully bedecked Christmas tree as a centerpiece. Advent calls us to consider these signs to be more than mere decorations. Thomas Merton spoke of things like Christmas trees, Advent wreaths and candles as sacraments—outward visible signs that confer grace, that bless us with the power of God's love. Merton believed that since God had become flesh in the world, the world and worldly things were precisely where we could find God.

In these days around Christmas, more than at any other time, our homes become churches. Delight your eyes and feast your soul on the various holiday sacraments in your home. Open your heart to the various graces they can confer. The Chinese proverb, "Keep a green tree in your heart and a singing bird will come" has an Advent twin: "Keep a green tree in your home and the Dove of God's love will come."

Saturday of the Third Week of Advent

When at communion you pray,
"Lord I am not worthy to receive you,
but only say the word and I shall be healed,"
Christ says, "More."

All true communion with Christ constantly requires more of us—more patience, more forgiveness, more generosity. Fortunately, the Bread of Life we receive at the eucharist also empowers us to be and do more. Likewise, our Advent conversion-construction has been a process of addition, enabling us to become more spiritually fit and confident, providing us many graces to help smooth out our rough ways. Yet, our Advent road is no pious by-pass around the messiness and disorder of daily life. Rather, the way passes directly through the tangled congestion of our human conflicts and dilemmas. Perhaps this is the reason apostolic followers of Jesus didn't call themselves Christians but members of "The Way." For them, conversion was a lifetime occupation in which there were no completed projects, and certainly no retirement.

Whatever you have achieved to this point in your Advent prayer and spiritual growth: it isn't sufficient. God wants more from you!

The Fourth Sunday of Advent

"Our birth is but a sleep and a forgetting."
—William Wordsworth

This last Advent Sunday tells of the coming of Christ in tender stories filled with all of the human anxieties and fears of young expectant parents. The child to be born of Mary was to be called "Emmanuel"—God is among us. Yet scholars say that Emmanuel is not so much a proper name as a victory cry. The joyous shout at the miracle of the birth of Jesus was "Emmanuel!" and for those with ears to hear, it is also the ecstatic cry heard at the miraculous birth of every child. Wordsworth poetically expressed this truth: "Trailing clouds of glory do we come from God, who is our home: heaven lies about in our infancy."

Every Christmas crèche is a shrine boldly proclaiming the wondrous glory of heaven that indeed surrounds every child's crib and infancy. As you gaze at your Christmas crèche, whisper Wordsworth's words: "Our birth is but a sleep and a forgetting." Then awaken to embrace the awesome mystery that Emmanuel is being born in you!

Monday of the Fourth Week of Advent

As you prepare for Christmas, be careful.

"**B**e careful," perhaps the most frequently given parental advice may also be the best advice for Advent. Be careful in this winter season not to catch a cold. Be careful when driving during this partying season, for highways can be dangerous. As you prepare for Christmas, being careful is not only the safe way; it's also the sacred way. Our way becomes truly smooth and holy when we are full of care, compassionately concerned for the needs of the poor. Be attentive to Advent's road sign: "Beware of being careless." When we are uncaring, anesthetized to the needs of the homeless and hungry, then we've lost our way on the Way.

In this season of gift-giving, make sure that under your Christmas tree are the invisible gifts you've already given away to our brothers and sisters in need.

Tuesday of the Fourth Week of Advent

"Life without wonder is not worth living."
—Rabbi Abraham Heschel

When being generous to the needs of the poor this Advent, don't forget your own poverty. The cause of our poverty is paradoxical: It is in the daily cascade of medical, scientific, and industrial miracles that we are sometimes paralyzed in our ability to wonder. Christmas is a magical season where glittering decorations and twinkling Christmas lights evoke wonder in small children—and occasionally even in numbed adults. "The world will never starve for wonders," G. K. Chesterton said, "but only for the want of wonder." Perhaps the best way to address this poverty is through prayer, for prayer opens us to wonder and wonder is the womb of worship.

Along with prayer, add another childlike quality to your preparation for Christmas: pretending. Even when you feel too old for this season, pretend to be in awe of the miraculous things all around you that are frequently disguised as the ordinary and common. If living in wonder becomes a habit, yours will be the best of all Christmas gifts—a wonder-full life.

Wednesday of the Fourth Week of Advent

"Thunderous Night, Holy Night!
Shepherds quake at the sight."

A foreign visitor unaccustomed to our Christmas traditions might be thunderstruck—truly amazed—to see a tall evergreen growing inside your house! And what a sight it is: a tree bejeweled with glistening ornaments and looped strings of flickering lights! Cleanse your eyes of convention to let your soul feast in awe at the vision of your Christmas tree; include a wish that your astonishment may awaken you to see all trees as full of wonder. Learn from your Christmas tree the wisdom that your soul is hungry in all seasons for a life and home decorated with enchanting beauty.

As the shepherds quaked at what they beheld, so may your soul quake as it hears the rumbling thunder of your seemingly silent Christmas tree! "Thunder?" you may ask. Indeed, the Latin word for astonishment literally means, "to thunder."

Thursday of the Fourth Week of Advent

"Handle with Care!"

To make this a most beautiful Christmas it might help to paste large red stickers that say, "Handle with care!" on all the gifts under your Christmas tree. These warning labels can be silent alarms reminding you to handle with care all your gifts: not just your possessions but also all your blessings, including your family, friends, neighbors, and even strangers. To "handle with care" requires attentive awareness to the preciousness of what is contained within your lovely flesh-wrapped gifts. To "handle with care" means treating all gifts of life with great reverence. This reverence flows not from guessing what's hidden inside your wrapped gifts, but from knowing that each of them holds the most precious presence of Christ.

In these whirling, revolving-door days just before Christmas, rudeness and impatience can easily cause you to mishandle—and so harm—your most treasured gifts. Remember to handle them with the greatest care.

Friday of the Fourth Week of Advent

"Make straight the crooked ways. Prepare the way of the Lord."

—The prophet Isaiah

As Christmas nears, we return to Advent's beginning and to your task of clearing away all obstacles to prepare the way of the Lord. During these Advent days you've labored to straighten out your crooked ways, to level your mountains of self-indulgence, and to smooth out all the rough spots in your relationships and spiritual life. Isn't it time now to rest and rejoice over your good labors? Not yet! For perhaps the greatest obstacle of all still remains: you!

After all your Advent labors, now comes the truly difficult task: allowing your reconstruction to come to its mysterious completion according to the divine blueprint by getting out of God's way. As motorists pull off to the side of the road for emergency vehicles, today give the "right of way" to God. When you yield to God's presence, you will begin to see the road sign "God At Work" written all along the way—especially in your unexpected hardships. Work with the Divine Engineer to reshape you in the divine image.

December 24th, Christmas Eve

"Joy to the world! The Lord is come . . . .
Let every heart prepare him room."

In story and song the most common emotion connected with this holiday is joy, yet sadly that blessed gift of the Spirit is often absent. Christmas is pregnant with promises of happy family gatherings and the joyful excitement of unwrapping gifts. Yet great expectations can lead to great disappointments! Isaac Watts' lyrics in the old Christmas carol reveal the secret of how to be happy this Holy Night and throughout the Twelve Days of Christmas: "Let every heart prepare him room." Unless we prepare by going inward to find God's joy in our heart, no person or thing that promises happiness can really make us happy.

This feast proclaims loudly that joy isn't reserved for heaven; it's a gift we begin to unwrap here in this life. Make Christmas a fusion feast: Let God's joyful presence within you be fused with the external expressions of Christmas delight. Let joy truly be born in your world this year.

December 25th, Christmas Day

"We wish you a Merry Christmas
and a Happy New Year."

For children young and old, this is the day when wishes come true. Adults need to keep in mind that 90 percent of a Merry Christmas is in our minds! Our thoughts, wishes, and attitudes have a powerful influence on creating a happy Christmas for others and in the process for ourselves as well. Sprinkled throughout the great tales of Christmas are gifts of magic wishes by which heroes and heroines make dreams come true. Magical wishes have enchanting power because they act as mental blueprints with the potential to shape the future.

Begin this Christmas Day by making three wishes: about the kind of person you want to be today, about the peaceful and joyful atmosphere you wish to create around you, and about the gifts of life and love you wish to share with your loved ones. Remember that the promise and power of your wishes is possible because of the great Gift we celebrate today. No Christmas is ever 100 percent free of unpleasant events or disappointments, but your wishes and dreams will give you the wondrous gift of a truly Merry Christmas.

Prepare the Way of the Lord

Gracious God,
   inspire us this Advent
   to make straight our ways
   so you can come to us and to our world.

Challenge us to fill in our valleys
   by increasing our deeds of charity,
   by expanding our times in prayer,
   and enlarging our gratitude for all your gifts.

Guide us with the light of your Spirit
   to be aware of the rough ways in our relationships
   with family, friends, and strangers,
   with co-workers, co-learners,
   and with those in authority.

Help us smooth out the bumps,
   and hills and mountains in the way.

Grant us patience as we pick away at Old Pride's Peak,
   our mountain of self-importance and selfishness.

With your grace may we become less,
   so that you can be more present in us.

May we carve out a space in ourselves
   where the Prince of Peace, the Wonder Counselor,
   can be born.

By all these Advent works
   may we prepare a roadway
   for a truly holy Christmas.
   Amen.